Locally made gown

Braided hair

A locally made hair

A nigerian made trouser suit

Nigerian made shoes

A blowse and wrapper often complimented with head ties

Nigerian made gowns

A traditional wear enhanced with neck beads and head tie

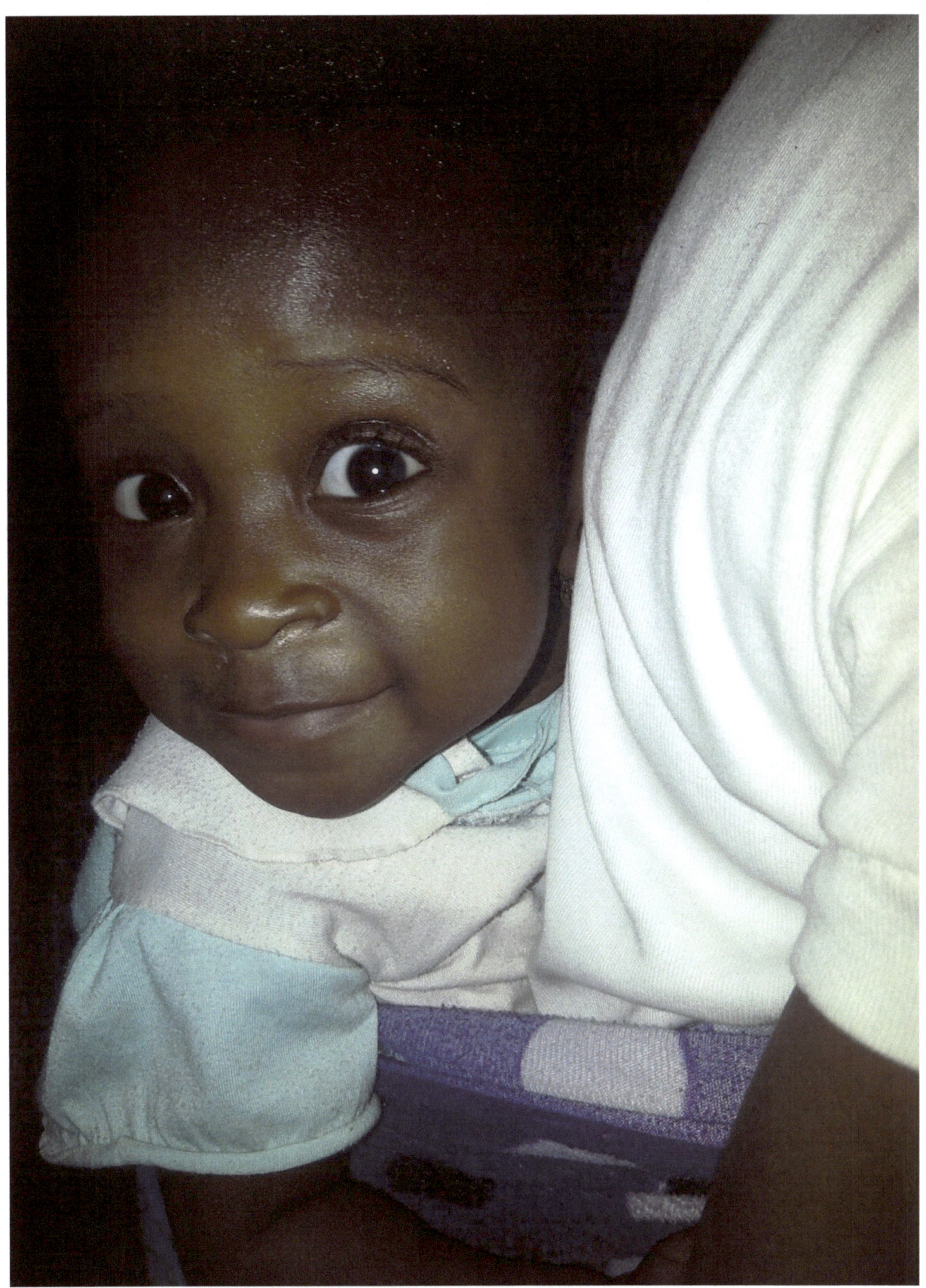

Traditional and convectional way of carrying babies on the back

Another view of an African woman

A well fitted gown made locally

Another view of the Nigerian made gown

A side view of a braided hair

A hand bag made with local cotton material called Ankara

Popular Men's wear known as Agbada

Another view of a Nigerian woman carrying a baby

A Nigerian made suit

A full length gown made in Nigeria

A skirt and blowse made with Ankara

Nigerian made gown

A gown made with a certain material called soaked in dyes and called Kampala

Nigerian dresses spiced up with neck beads

Another view of women's gown

Carrying a baby on the back can be fashionable